THE CREATIVE CURRICULUM®
LearningGames®

12–24 Months

Joseph Sparling and Isabelle Lewis

Foreword by Diane Trister Dodge

This book of *LearningGames* is being shared with the family of

_____

Teaching Strategies® Inc.
Washington, DC

Editor: Kai-leé Berke
Design: Carla Uriona
Layout/production: Tony MacFarlane and Abner Nieves

Published by:
Teaching Strategies, Inc.
P.O. Box 42243
Washington, DC 20015
www.TeachingStrategies.com

ISBN: 978-1-933021-59-1

Printed and bound in the United States of America

2012	2011	2010	2009	2008	2007
6	5	4	3	2	1

Contents

THE CREATIVE CURRICULUM®
LearningGames®

Foreword

Dear Parents,

It gives me great pleasure to introduce you to an exciting program called *The Creative Curriculum® LearningGames®*. The games are designed to build the kinds of skills that lead to successful, lifelong learning for your child. You are the key to making this happen.

On a regular basis you will be receiving a colorful handout describing simple and fun games to play with your child. They don't require any special toys or materials. You can do them as part of your everyday experiences with your child. But they can make a big difference, and they already have made a difference for thousands of children and families.

There are five different sets of *LearningGames* for children of different ages. You will receive only the games appropriate for your child. It's never too soon to start. Right from birth, your child is learning and growing. The experiences you provide during the first 5 years of life will help to build your child's brain, develop thinking skills, promote social skills, and build your child's confidence as a learner.

You are your child's first and most important teacher. Everything you do with your child, everything you say, every song you sing, and every object you give your child to play with teach important lessons. One of the wonderful results of using these games is that they help you to build a positive relationship with your child. And as your child is learning, you are as well. You will gain an understanding of child development and many practical ideas for guiding your child's learning.

Many programs using the *LearningGames* are also implementing either *The Creative Curriculum® for Infants, Toddlers & Twos* or *The Creative Curriculum® for Preschool*. As the lead author on these comprehensive curriculum materials, I am very excited to be able to offer this parent component, too. Children benefit the most when the important adults in their lives—their parents, caregivers, teachers, health care specialists, or home visitors—are working together to support their learning and growth.

I wish you great enjoyment and success,

Diane Trister Dodge
President
Teaching Strategies, Inc.

Acknowledgments

Many people helped in the preparation of *The Creative Curriculum®* *LearningGames®*. We would like to thank Kai-leé Berke and Heather Baker for their thoughtful writing contributions and for finding wonderful children's books that enhance each game. Thank you to Nancy Guadagno, Sharon Samber, Toni Bickart, and Rachel Tickner, our editors, for their attention to detail. We appreciate the work of Carla Uriona, who designed the new format for the activities, and Abner Nieves and Tony MacFarlane for their careful layout work. Thanks to Nancy Guadagno and Kai-leé Berke for their patience and persistence in moving the writing, editing, and production process forward.

Checklist for
The Creative Curriculum® LearningGames®:
12-24 months

I have shared the LearningGames *checked below with the family of* _____

Given to Family	*LearningGames* Activity Number and Title	Date Given to Family/Notes
☐	35. Let's Clean Up	
☐	36. Pointing and Naming	
☐	37. Animal Sounds	
☐	38. Making Lines	
☐	39. Touch and Name With Books	
☐	40. Roll the Ball	
☐	41. Learning to Predict	
☐	42. Make Undressing Easy	
☐	43. Touch Your Toes	
☐	44. Talking About Feelings	
☐	45. Water Play	
☐	46. Hide-and-Seek	
☐	47. Action Words	
☐	48. Low Jump	
☐	49. Sing Together	
☐	50. Nesting Objects	

Given to Family	LearningGames Activity Number and Title	Date Given to Family/Notes
☐	51. Blow Things	
☐	52. Matching Shapes and Sizes	
☐	53. Build Together	
☐	54. Cardboard Boxes	
☐	55. Talking Throughout the Day	
☐	56. Expressing Needs	
☐	57. Sorting Shapes	
☐	58. Choosing Lids	
☐	59. Beginning to Share	
☐	60. Exploring Outdoors	
☐	61. How Does It Feel?	
☐	62. Painting With Water	
☐	63. Scribbling	
☐	64. Trying New Motions	
☐	65. Matching Colors	
☐	66. Using Tools	
☐	67. See, Show, Say	

What Your Child May Be Doing
One-Year-Olds (12–24 Months)

Social/Emotional Development

Find new ways to make things happen

Follow simple requests and understand more language than they can express

Are increasingly aware of their possessions

Become aware of others' expressions of emotions

Enjoy realistic toys (for example, baby dolls, bottles, cradles, and telephones)

Initiate peek-a-boo activities

Cognitive Development

Make choices between clear alternatives

Begin to solve problems

Learn by moving and doing

Concentrate for longer periods of time

Learn how to open doors and flip light switches

Enjoy sorting and nesting toys

Physical Development

Pull themselves to standing and cruise by holding on to furniture

Walk steadily, but may prefer to crawl

Use carts, baby carriages, and other wheeled toys to support walking

Begin to climb and slide

Move rhythmically to music

Clap

Take objects out and put them back in containers; fill and dump

Roll and throw balls

Reach successfully for moving objects (for example, bubbles)

Start to stack objects

Language and Literacy Development

Follow simple requests and understand more language than they can express

Use gestures and sounds to communicate

Wave good-bye

Understand and respond to many words, simple directions, and questions

Increase expressive vocabulary

Hold crayons and make marks on paper

Learn to turn pages

Point to familiar pictures in a book

THE CREATIVE CURRICULUM®
LearningGames®

Let's Clean Up

You're putting the rattle in your basket.

Make clean-up time a game by naming the toys your child chooses to put in the clean-up basket.

Having choices during clean-up time may make it easier for your child to learn about taking care of his belongings.

Why this is important

Giving your child a chance to make choices during play and cleanup helps him learn about taking care of his things. When the choices he makes during simple tasks bring a positive result, such as helping you, he gains trust in his own ability to make decisions. As he has opportunities to make more choices, he builds confidence and independence.

What you do

- Invite your child to help you clean up toys after playing. At this age, don't expect him to really clean up things by himself. Sit beside him, show him a container such as a toy box or basket, and drop in one of his toys. Talk about what you are doing. *It's time to put the toys away. Mommy put the car in the basket.*

- Hand him a toy and ask him to put it in the basket. If he does not drop it, help him release it into the basket. Then, hand him the toy again and let him have another try.

- Repeat the game until he understands what you want him to do. Offer encouraging words when he drops the toy in the basket. *You put the ball away!*

- Invite him to choose a toy to put in the basket. If he chooses an object not intended for the basket, give him another place to put it. *Only toys go in the basket. You can put the magazine on the table.*

- Talk about each toy as it goes in the basket. As he has more practice with cleaning up, count the toys as he puts them away. *One, two, three. You put three green cars in the basket!*

Another idea

Use different containers for storage to give your child more choices. Try putting toys away in a large plastic bowl, a shopping bag, an egg carton, or a backpack.

Let's read together!

I'm Dirty!
by Kate and Jim McMullan

Pointing and Naming

Look at that big dog over there.

Point to things as you name them for your child, and name the things your child points to.

Purposely pointing out objects, both near and far, helps your child to notice those things and gradually learn their names.

THE
CREATIVE CURRICULUM®
LearningGames®

Copyright 2007 Joseph Sparling

Why this is important

You can guide your child's attention by pointing to objects he may not notice. Pointing and gesturing help him begin to understand direction. Starting now and continuing throughout his life, body language and pointing will help him communicate.

What you do

- Point out interesting and useful objects during the time you spend with your child. For example, when he is looking for his toy truck, point to the truck and say *Truck. There is your truck*. Wait to see if he notices the truck before you walk over and touch it to get his attention.

- Show him everyday objects outside his home such as birds at a birdfeeder or cars driving by. Point to high clouds, airplanes, or blowing leaves. Point to faraway lights, signs, or people walking.

- Always name the objects as you point to them.

- If your child makes any attempt to point, smile and talk about what he sees. *Kitty. You're showing me the kitty!*

Ready to move on?

As you point to something say, *Look at that*. Do not immediately name it. Instead, ask a question. *What do you think it is?* Pause before giving the answer. *That's a butterfly.*

Let's read together!

Bright Baby Trucks
by Roger Priddy

Animal Sounds

The dog says woof, woof!

Make a sound for an animal toy and see if your child can imitate the sound or point to a picture of that animal.

Your child will begin to connect animals with their sounds and their pictures.

THE
CREATIVE CURRICULUM®
Learning Games®
Copyright 2007 Joseph Sparling

Why this is important

Animal names and sounds are useful information in your child's expanding world, and imitating those sounds can be fun. Playing the game with a toy animal and a picture of that same animal helps your child understand that a picture can represent an object. Later, seeing letters next to the animal pictures will help your child to understand that letters stand for sounds.

What you do

- Name one of your child's animal toys and make the sound that animal makes. *This is a dog. The dog says woof!* Repeat the sound and encourage your child to make dog sounds.

- Add a new animal to the game periodically until he knows several animals and their sounds.

- Show him a picture of an animal he knows while also showing him the toy. Remove the toy and point to the picture. Ask him what sound it makes. He may not immediately connect the sound with the picture. *This is the cat. What does a cat say?*

Ready to move on?

Help your child learn the word for the animal as well as the sound the animal makes by repeating the name a couple of times and making the sound. *Dog. Dog. A dog says woof, woof!* Acknowledge any attempts your child makes to say the word. For example, if your child said *Doh, doh,* you might say, *Dog! You are saying dog!*

Let's read together!

Old MacDonald
by Rosemary Wells

Making Lines

You made a long, straight line!

Describe the marks your child makes with his fingers or a stick.

This encourages your child's awareness of the many kinds of marks that he can later use in drawing or writing.

Why this is important

Children enjoy making marks. With practice, he will become aware of the feeling of his hands and arms as they draw lines. He will begin to notice and feel the differences among the marks he makes. Pointing out the shapes of lines helps him see the variations he has accidentally made happen. These steps will help him when he begins to use his hands for more complex tasks such as controlled scribbling, drawing, or writing.

What you do

- Talk about what your child is doing when you notice him tracing his finger over a flat surface. *You are making a wiggly line.* Trace your finger beside his line and tell him you are making a wiggly line like his.

- Look for interesting places around the house to practice making lines. Trace lines with your child on a steamy window or mirror. Talk about what he makes. *That is a straight line. That line is curved.*

- Show him how to spread his fingers apart and make a series of lines or make a fist and create a wide stroke. When playing outside, show him how to use a stick to draw in the sandbox, dirt, or mud.

Another idea

Put a few cups of sand in a baking dish. Encourage your child to use his fingers to make lines in the sand.

Let's read together!

When a Line Bends…A Shape Begins
by Rhonda Gowler Greene

Touch and Name With Books

You pointed to the baby's hat!

Name any picture your child touches in a book.

Talking about the things your child touches helps him learn the names of things he finds interesting.

THE
CREATIVE CURRICULUM®
LearningGames®
Copyright 2007 Joseph Sparling

Why this is important

You can follow your child's lead and give him information about the pictures he notices in a book. By naming the things he touches or points to, you are talking about something that already has his interest. Later he can show you he knows the names of pictures by pointing to them when you ask him to.

What you do

- Point to the pictures as you name them when sharing a book with your child. Keep the activity simple by pointing to one object per page, slowly naming each one.

- Wait until your child touches something on the page. Then name and talk about that thing. *You're touching the pig.*

- Listen to hear if your child says something that sounds a little like *What's that?* as he points. Repeat his attempted words and immediately answer. *What's that? It's an airplane.*

- Ask him a question to encourage him to point to something, if he does not touch anything on the page. *What do you like on this page?*

Ready to move on?

When your child becomes familiar with the book, encourage him to point to things you name in the pictures. *Can you show me the puppy? There it is!* You can also play the game with picture cards or with posters on the wall.

Let's read together!

Good Night, Baby
by Cheryl Willis Hudson
and George Ford

Roll the Ball

Can you roll the ball to me?

Roll a soft ball back and forth with your child and tell him he is taking turns.

You will be introducing your child to a simple game that requires cooperation and turn-taking.

THE
CREATIVE CURRICULUM®
LearningGames®
Copyright 2007 Joseph Sparling

Why this is important

With this game, you help your child understand that some things work better with a partner. He will learn that being a partner means you must give sometimes (roll) in order to get back (catch). Rolling a ball back and forth teaches a very easy form of cooperation. Knowing how to cooperate will prepare your child to enter into more complex kinds of play with other children later on.

What you do

● Sit with your toddler on the floor facing each other with your legs spread and your legs close to his so that the ball cannot escape.

● Roll the ball slowly so that he is sure to catch it.

● Talk to him about rolling it back. He may not want to roll the ball back to you. *Roll the ball to me so I can roll it to you again!* If he still refuses, gently take the ball and quickly roll it to him. You may have to repeat this process several times before he understands that he is not losing the ball when he rolls it away.

● Respond positively about the game you are now playing together when he rolls the ball back to you. *You rolled the ball to me and I rolled it back to you. We're taking turns!*

Ready to move on?

As he gains better control of the ball, sit farther apart to challenge him. If your child stands up and throws the ball toward you, he may be ready to try an easy throwing game.

Let's read together!

Ten Black Dots
by Donald Crews

Learning to Predict

Where will the ball go?

Toss a ball into a big box or roll it through a tube and then invite your child to look for the ball.

Repeating the game gives your child experience in predicting the outcome of his actions.

THE CREATIVE CURRICULUM®
LearningGames®

Copyright 2007 Joseph Sparling

Why this is important

When you repeat a simple activity, your child will begin to anticipate what will happen because he has seen it happen before. Repeating the process of throwing a ball into a box helps your child learn to predict where to find an object that has gone from sight. Doing the game again and again helps him learn that he can act in a particular way with an expected result. This builds your child's self-confidence.

What you do

- Find a soft ball and a big box. Stand with your child several feet from the box and throw the ball into it. Ask, *Where did the ball go? Do you see it?*

- Encourage him to look into the box if he does not understand what you are asking.

- Wait for him to notice the ball, and respond with pleasure at his discovery. Repeat this process several times.

- Next, give the child a chance to throw the ball into the box from a few feet away. Respond with enthusiasm each time the ball is found.

Another idea

Try the game using a smaller ball and a tube. Hold the tube higher at one end. Invite your toddler to put the ball in the higher end of the tube. Guide his attention as you play. *There goes the ball! It's coming through the tube.* At first, he may look into the tube to find the ball. After a few times, he will begin to expect the ball to appear at the other end. Hold the tube in different ways to make the ball move fast or slow.

Let's read together!

Peek-a-Who?
by Nina Laden

Make Undressing Easy

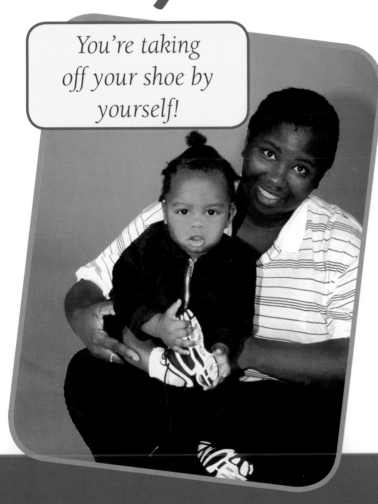

You're taking off your shoe by yourself!

Loosen your child's shoes, unzip his coat, or pull his shirt partly over his head so he can do the last part of the action.

Your child will have the satisfaction of successfully completing the job of removing clothes.

Why this is important

Undressing is a basic part of caring for one's own needs and moving toward independence. Your child may want to undress himself before he has the skills and he may not want you to help him. As he practices this new type of independence, he will be more willing to accept help if he feels he is accomplishing part of it on his own.

- Choose a part of the day when you have plenty of time for your child to practice undressing. It is best if you can make time to practice during a natural undressing transition, such as before a bath or taking off shoes when he comes inside.

- Start with his shoes, because most children are interested first in removing those. Untie the laces and loosen the shoe at his heel so that he only needs to pull it off his toes. Prepare the socks the same way by removing them from most of his foot before he pulls them off.

- Offer positive feedback after each item of clothing is removed. *You took off your shoe! I think you can pull off your sock, too!*

- Undo any buttons or zippers and show him how to pull his arm through the sleeve, when your child is ready to try more difficult pieces of clothing such as a coat or shirt.

- Help with pants by having your child stand and push his pants down to his knees. Then have him sit and invite him to pull them over his feet by himself.

Another idea

Talk about the patterns and colors on his clothes. As he takes off each item, use their names to help teach him the words to describe his clothing. *Red shirt. You are taking off your red shirt.*

Let's read together!

All By Myself
by Mercer Mayer

Touch Your Toes

Touch your toes.

Invite your child to touch parts of her body while you touch and name yours.

Your child will learn about herself and better understand the name that goes with each body part.

Why this is important

When your child learns the names of her body parts she is getting to know herself better. By repeating the name several times, you encourage her to try to say the name. In naming and locating the various parts of her body, your child becomes more aware of herself as an individual.

What you do

- Touch your ears while saying: *I'm touching my ears. Can you touch your ears?* In the beginning, choose familiar parts such as ears, tummy, or toes.

- Give her plenty of time to respond, and repeat the word if needed. She will follow your lead but may be slower in touching the right spot because she has to see where it is first. If she needs help, gently guide her hands to the body part.

- Invite her to lead the game as you name the parts after she points to them. This gives her a chance to hear the words for those parts she may not know the names of yet.

- Encourage her to repeat the word as she points to that part of her body. *Tummy. You are pointing to your tummy. Can you say* tummy?

Another idea

Turn the game into a song that involves body movement. Try a simple version of "Looby-Loo" or "Hokey Pokey." You can add new verses as she learns the words for more body parts.

Let's read together!

From Head to Toe
by Eric Carle

Talking About Feelings

You're smiling. I can tell you feel happy.

You're sad. You really want your blanket.

Watch your child's facial expressions and body language and then describe her feelings for her.

Your child may begin to learn that words, as well as actions, can help explain what she feels.

THE
CREATIVE CURRICULUM®
LearningGames®

Why this is important

When your baby was very young, you made a point of letting her see feelings expressed on your face. Now you can help her by giving her words as well as facial expressions. It may take time for her to know the correct words for each emotion. When she has words for her feelings, she will have a choice between words and actions for expression. Both will help her in making her feelings known to others.

What you do

- Watch for moments when your child feels strongly about something, and then describe her emotions for her. For example, when she jumps up and down at the sight of a bunch of balloons you might say, *You're so excited to see those balloons!*

- Help her calm down when she feels very sad, annoyed, or angry by describing her intense emotions and showing her with your facial expressions and tone of voice that you understand what she is feeling. *You are really sad that Daddy just left. You love him so much.*

- Describe her emotions in calmer times too. *I see your little smile. You are happy to see your teddy.*

Another idea

Use many words to describe her feelings such as *frustrated, annoyed, disappointed, bored, amazed, calm,* and *relaxed.* Hearing many feeling words will help her be able to identify and name her specific feelings as she gets older.

Let's read together!

Llama, Llama Red Pajama
by Anna Dewdney

Water Play

> *The soap feels slippery, doesn't it?*

Without directing him, invite your child to play with water while you say what is happening.

Your child may understand the meaning of most of your words when they describe exactly what he is doing as he does it.

THE
CREATIVE CURRICULUM®
LearningGames®
Copyright 2007 Joseph Sparling

Why this is important

Young children enjoy water because it moves in unexpected ways. Talking about your child's actions as he plays with water can help him understand the meaning of your words because he can relate them to what he is doing.

What you do

- During bath time, give your child a few toys and talk about everything he sees and touches. *The duck makes a splash when you drop him. The soap is making bubbles on your tummy! See how the warm water goes drip-drip-drip from the faucet?*

- When playing outside, give him a dishpan partly filled with water. Offer him a few toys and plastic cups to play with. Talk about his actions. *You poured water into that cup until it overflowed. You have two hands in the water. You're smiling. I think playing in the water makes you happy.*

Another idea

Find other opportunities for water play. Let him play with water in the sink as you wash dishes, or let him linger for a moment in the soapy water after washing his hands. Talk about what he is doing.

Let's read together!

Splash!
by Sarah Garland

Hide-and-Seek

Oh! You found me!

Move partly out of sight and let your child find you.

Hide-and-seek encourages your child to move around and rely on her own ability to find something that is hidden.

Why this is important

Learning to look for objects she cannot see gives your child a new tool for problem solving. Playing hide-and-seek helps her independently find something out of sight and introduces her to a simple game that she will be able to play later on with other children.

What you do

● Tell your toddler you are going to hide, and then duck down behind a chair or move to another part of the room so that you are almost out of sight. Let her see you go.

● Call, *Can you find me? Where am I?* Offer positive feedback when she finds you and give her a big hug. *You are so smart! You found me!*

● Play together for as long as she is interested. Hide in new places to keep her attention.

● Offer her a chance to hide, and ask loudly, *Where's Carla? Where did she go?* She may hide in the same place you hid. When you find her, act surprised and hug her close.

Ready to move on?

When she is a little older, try playing the game by hiding a stuffed animal in another room. Do not let her see you hide it, but place the toy where she will easily see it. Go back to her and ask, *Where is teddy? Can you help me find him?* Point or give any help your child needs. Show surprise when she finds the toy. *Wow! You found him in the kitchen!*

Let's read together!

Open the Barn Door, Find a Cow
by Christopher Santoro

Action Words

Spread your arms wide!

Describe what is happening while you and your child move in interesting ways.

By hearing or saying the words while doing the movement, your child will be likely to learn action words.

We can stand on our heads.

THE
CREATIVE CURRICULUM®
LearningGames®
Copyright 2007 Joseph Sparling

Why this is important

Attaching labels to your child's actions helps her begin to recognize the words for what she is doing. Learning the words takes longer than learning the motions, but she will enjoy practicing. In the early stages of using words, your child may have difficulty understanding what the words mean. Acting them out helps her learn their meanings.

What you do

- Imitate your child's movements and talk about the action as she tumbles or rolls around on the floor. *We're rolling over. You're standing on your head.*

- Suggest new actions to try, and remember to give her words for what you are doing. *Move your hands up and down. Bend over. Spread your arms wide.*

- Try these movements with your child:

    Stand on your toes with your arms stretched high and say: *Reach high.*

    Squat, tuck in your head, hold your knees, and say: *Make a ball.*

    Lie on your back with your feet in the air and say: *Feet up.*

    Turn around quickly and say: *Spin.*

Ready to move on?

As your child gains more control of her body, add more challenging motions such as jumping and standing on one foot.

Let's read together!

All Fall Down
by Helen Oxenbury

Low Jump

That's a big jump!

Invite your child to jump from a low place while you hold on to him.

Your child will have a safe way to try a new skill and feel confident about moving his body.

THE
CREATIVE CURRICULUM®
LearningGames®
Copyright 2007 Joseph Sparling

Why this is important

Now that your child walks well, he will enjoy learning new ways to move. Some children take longer to feel comfortable jumping, but if your child is allowed to progress at his own pace, he will be more willing to practice. If you plan for his safety and success, your child will gain confidence about moving his body in new ways.

What you do

- Help your child stand on a low stool or bottom step. **Only choose low places for your child to jump from. Remain with your child while he practices.**

- Hold him under his arms, help him jump to the floor, and say *Jump!* Lift him higher than necessary to help him feel the motion.

- Repeat this activity until he feels comfortable and confident with jumping.

- Give him the chance to jump while only holding onto your hands. Let him maintain his balance, but use your hands to help support him.

- Talk to him about safety during the activity: *We only jump from low places.*

Another idea

Use a board to set up a small ramp that your child can walk up and down. Help him jump down at the end. Lay the board on the floor and show him how to jump over it. Use the words *up*, *down*, and *over* to talk about the movements. Also, you can hold hands and jump around the room, or imitate animals such as frogs, rabbits, or kangaroos.

Let's read together!

Baby Dance
by Ann Taylor

Sing Together

Clap, clap, clap with me!

Sing songs with your child, especially ones that she can clap to or that have her name in them.

Singing provides a fun and interesting way to teach your child words and sound patterns.

Why this is important

Your child will become familiar with words, especially rhyming words, through the rhythm and repetition of singing. By hearing the repeated sounds in songs like "Row, Row, Row Your Boat," she will become familiar with the patterns of sounds that occur in language. Singing crosses all language barriers, and when done in a group, singing provides your child with social experiences.

What you do

● Sing with your child when feeding, dressing, walking, or riding. Sometimes use traditional songs and sometimes make up your own. Remember that your child does not care if you sing well. She will enjoy hearing your voice in songs about her and her activities.

● Clap and invite your child to clap with you. Choose a simple, repetitious tune that your child can sing with you and clap to the rhythm. *Row, row, row your boat, gently down the stream. Merrily, merrily, merrily, merrily, life is but a dream.* Your child will first listen, and then begin to imitate the sounds she hears. She may clap and move to the tune before she tries to sing.

● Make up a song with your child's name in it. *Lucy, Lucy, Lucy Ann. I really love you. Lucy, Lucy, Lucy Ann. I really love you* (sung to the tune of "Row, Row, Row Your Boat").

● Try to remember songs your parents sang to you and share them with your child. If your family speaks more than one language, this can be a great way to pass on family traditions.

Another idea

Look for picture books at the library that are based on the words to your child's favorite songs. Sing the song and then read the book together.

Let's read together!

Skip To My Lou
by Nadine Bernard Westcott

Nesting Objects

You're putting the small cup in the big one!

While your child plays with objects that fit together, ask questions and talk about what she is doing.

Your child may begin to recognize differences in size and will become familiar with size words.

Why this important

By offering her materials of different sizes, you draw her attention to some of the ways objects may fit together. Hearing you describe her actions, she learns words such as big, bigger, small, and smaller. Putting things in order and understanding sizes prepares your child for certain kinds of math learning later in life. As she grows she will use this knowledge to understand ideas such as first, second, and third.

What you do

- Offer your child various household containers in graduated sizes such as juice cans, measuring cups, or plastic storage dishes. Set them in front of her, and then step back and watch her explore them. She may roll, bang, or hide them.

- Give positive feedback when she nests two or more objects. *Look! You put one cup inside the other.*

- Ask her questions about a set of cups by holding the largest one and asking her which one goes in next. Do not correct her if she chooses the wrong cup. Let her experiment with the different sizes.

- Use words to describe the various containers. *That cup is big and this one is small. The small cup is green. The big cup is red.*

- If she appears frustrated, make the game simple by only offering the largest and smallest containers.

Another idea

Look around the house for objects that nest together such as cardboard boxes and plastic bowls. Watch her as she figures out the best way to put items together.

Let's read together!

Blueberry Shoe
by Ann Dixon

Blow Things

You're blowing a bubble!

Let your child discover that she can move light objects by blowing on them.

You will be introducing your child to a new way to experiment with cause and effect.

Why this is important

Blowing an object produces an unusual result that your child may not be used to. She will see that different objects react in different ways to the same action. Your child will enjoy the control she has over an object, such as a bubble wand or a straw, through this simple cause-and-effect game.

What you do

- Introduce your child to purposeful blowing by saying, *Blow* and then gently blowing against her cheek or hair.

- Pucker your mouth and blow through a bubble wand so she can see the bubbles forming. Let her try. At first, she may suck in air instead of blowing out.

- Provide many opportunities for her to practice blowing until she masters the skill.

- Offer her simple items to blow against such as a feather, water, plastic ball, or bits of paper. Tell her about the effect of her actions. *You made ripples in the water! You are blowing the ball across the table!* **Only allow your child to use whistles, straws, and other small things while you are watching. When you are not directly supervising your child's play, remove anything that is small enough for your child to swallow or long enough to injure the back of your child's throat.**

Another idea

Offer her noise-making objects to practice with. A horn, whistle, or party blower will produce a loud noise that will delight your child. Puff out your cheeks to blow through the noisemaker and then let your child try. *You blew into the horn and it made a loud sound!*

Let's read together!

Bubbles, Bubbles
by Kathi Appelt

Matching Shapes and Sizes

Can you find one like mine?

Help your child notice two things that match in a set of three items.

Your child may begin to pay closer attention to similarities and differences.

THE CREATIVE CURRICULUM®
LearningGames®

Copyright 2007 Joseph Sparling

Why this is important

This game will help your child notice the similarities and differences in objects. When asked to choose or identify an object, she must focus on an item's identifying features (hard, soft, round, straight, big, small, etc.). Noticing these special features helps your child recognize new objects and compare them to things she has seen before. Practicing with three-dimensional objects that she can hold and explore will also help prepare her to notice the distinctive features of two-dimensional items such as letters on a page.

What you do

- Offer your toddler three objects of the same size and color. Two of them should be the same shape, such as two yellow balls and a yellow block. Talk about each object she picks up. *That is a smooth, round ball. It's yellow.* Point out the two similar objects.

- Pick up one of the two similar objects and hold it up for her to see. Ask her to find the other one. *Can you find one like this?* When she finds it, hold your hand next to hers so that she can see the objects together.

- Provide encouragement if she chooses the different object. *You found the one that is different. This other one is like mine. See, it's round.*

- Speak lovingly each time she chooses, even if she chooses the object that doesn't match. At first she may choose randomly until she understands the game. Give her many opportunities to play.

Another idea

Some items that work well for matching shapes are: spoons and forks, balls and blocks, or round and square plastic lids. To practice with items of varying sizes, try big and little spoons, plastic cups, or socks.

Let's read together!

Mouse Shapes
by Ellen Stoll Walsh

Build Together

I made my blocks just like yours.

While building with blocks and other materials, copy what your child builds and later invite her to follow your lead.

Your child may become more aware of patterns and learn that patterns can be repeated or varied.

Here are some other things we can build with.

Why this is important

When you copy something your child builds, you help her notice and learn about patterns. Describing what you are doing as you copy her gives her language to describe her actions. If she wants to use the blocks to build what you are building, she will need to listen to words that give directions. Gaining directions from words is an important skill that she will use throughout her life.

What you do

- Sit with your child and invite her to join you in playing with blocks. Arrange the blocks so that you both have a few to play with. Make sure your blocks are similar to hers.

- Encourage your child to begin building with her blocks, and then copy her movements. Talk about what you are doing. *I'm putting my long block on its side, just like you did.*

- Point out similarities between the two finished structures.

- Let your child choose her blocks, and do not insist that she imitate you or build in a particular way. At first, she may not sit still for the game or fully understand what you are asking her to do.

- Invite her to be the leader again, and this time ask for direction as you play. *What block should I use next?*

- Make the game challenging by giving her directions to follow as you build a specific object such as a train. *Let's each make a train.* Build your structure slowly from left to right, and ask her to find each block that you use. *Find your big green block and that will be the engine.*

Another idea

Look for other materials to use for a shared activity. You could string a necklace together or build a fence with sticks. Any matched set of items will work.

Let's read together!

Hands Can
by Cheryl Willis Hudson

Cardboard Boxes

What a cozy house you have!

Observe your child as she plays with boxes, and occasionally describe what she is doing.

Allowing your child to play freely gives her the chance to plan her own experience and use her imagination.

Why this is important

Your child needs opportunities to plan her play and create her own spaces. A cardboard box provides a place for active and quiet play. When she can make choices about her play she will feel good about herself and her ability to make decisions. She may also benefit from the secluded space the box provides.

What you do

- Give your child a box in a place where she has plenty of room to play with it. Before play, examine the boxes. **Don't use boxes with staples. Remove any small, loose pieces of paper, cardboard, or other packing materials. During play, watch to be sure that your child doesn't tear off anything that she might put in her mouth and choke on.**

- Lay the box on its side if it is too tall for her to step into. If she gets in the box but cannot get out, gently tip it over so she can crawl out.

- Notice how she manipulates a small box by putting it on her head or filling it with toys. With a large box, she may enjoy sitting peacefully inside, tipping it over, or climbing on it.

- Talk to her about her movements using the words *in, under, on,* or *out.*

- Allow her to explore without direction, but offer help if needed.

Another idea

Look for boxes with words printed on them. If she notices the letters, trace them with your finger and talk to her about what the letters say. *This says* bananas *because bananas were in this box.*

Let's read together!

The Birthday Box
by Leslie Patricelli

Talking Throughout the Day

See the pretty flower?

Talk to your child frequently throughout the day, naming objects and describing his actions.

Your child will learn many words and may notice the many ways that words are used.

Why this is important

Letting your child hear specific words for objects and actions helps him understand the purpose of language. He will better understand simple words that are directly related to his actions. He is less likely to understand when given a long sentence. Offering a word or two to describe his actions will help him link the word to its meaning. When he knows what certain words mean, he will begin to practice saying them.

What you do

- Speak to your child with simple sentences and specific language. Instead of saying, *Bring me your things, please,* try saying, *Please bring me your shoes.*

- Offer verbal feedback as he completes the task. *You brought your blue shoes.* Talk about what you expect him to do and what he has just done.

- Replace phrases such as *Let's go* with more specific language. *Let's take a ride in the car.* Use the same specific language when offering encouragement. *You climbed in the car all by yourself!*

- Repeat his own words back to him in simple sentences to give him a pattern for speech. When he says, *Flower,* try to understand what he is trying to say, and expand on his words. *Yes. I see the pretty, yellow flower.*

Ready to move on?

As he understands more words, offer more complex instructions such as: *Please put your blue ball in the toy box.*

Let's read together!

My Love For You
by Susan L. Roth

Expressing Needs

You're hungry. You need your cereal.

Talk to your child about what he needs.

Giving him words to express his needs gradually develops his ability to tell you what he needs and wants.

THE CREATIVE CURRICULUM®
LearningGames®

Copyright 2007 Joseph Sparling

Why this is important

By giving your child the words to express his needs, you help him begin to understand that he needs certain things in certain situations. When you ask him about his needs, he has the opportunity to use gestures and simple words to express himself. The more words he can use to clearly express his needs, the more likely his needs will be met.

What you do

- Give your child words to describe his needs. Help your child talk about what he sees and experiences. Here are a few examples:

    You need a spoon for your cereal. I'll get it for you.

    You need a bath before bedtime. Can you find your rubber boat?

    You need a warm coat to go out today. It's cold outside.

- Guess what his needs are by observing his gestures and body language. When he looks or points at an object, try to put his action into words to show him you are trying to understand. *Do you need the doll?* He will appreciate your effort to understand and help him.

- Notice when he begins to use simple words such as *cold* or *hungry* to let you know what he needs. Respond to him quickly to let him know you understand.

Ready to move on?

You can encourage your child to talk about his own needs by asking questions. *Do you have something to put your sand in? How can you reach that high shelf? Would you like me to hold you?*

Let's read together!

Big Dog & Little Dog
by Dav Pilkey

Sorting Shapes

You're putting the ball in the round hole.

Talk to your child about shapes as she sorts objects into containers.

Your child will begin to recognize and understand the similarities and differences between objects.

THE
CREATIVE CURRICULUM®
LearningGames®
Copyright 2007 Joseph Sparling

Why this is important

When your child practices picking up and sorting objects, she gains hand-eye coordination by manipulating the toys and judging each characteristic she sees. As she plays and you describe the objects she sorts, she gains an understanding of basic shapes. As she gets older, that understanding will help her recognize the straight and curved lines of letters in reading and writing.

What you do

- Give your child one or two balls to drop into a wide-mouthed container such as an oatmeal box. Keep the game very simple to start. Notice how she drops a ball in, listens for the *clunk* of it hitting the bottom, and then dumps it out again.

- Offer her two containers when she seems ready for more variety. Prepare each container with a different-shaped hole in the lid, such as a square opening and a round opening. Give her a few blocks to go with the balls she already has.

- Show your child how the block fits in the square hole and the ball fits in the round hole, or wait to see if she tries it herself.

- Encourage her to continue when she successfully drops in a block.
  You fit the block into the square hole! Now can you put the ball in the round hole?

- Offer help if your child appears frustrated. Add more shapes to the game only after she becomes skilled at sorting one or two shapes.

Another idea

Offer your child only the lids and containers to play with. Help her use her finger to trace the holes on each lid as you talk about the shape. *This lid has a square hole with straight sides and corners.*

Let's read together!

Bear in a Square
by Stella Blackstone

Choosing Lids

You found a lid that fits just right!

Offer your child a variety of jars with screw-on lids and talk about what he's doing as he experiments with them.

Your child will practice turning the lids to open and close them and may begin to make thoughtful choices about which lid to use for each jar.

Why this is important

Giving your child the opportunity to experiment with containers and screw-on lids encourages him to use a trial-and-error approach to solving a problem. When given choices, your child may choose randomly at first. However, through repetition, he will begin to develop problem-solving skills and make more selective choices. This activity also encourages him to coordinate his hands to help him select and screw on the lids.

What you do

- Show your child a plastic container with a screw-on lid. Slowly unscrew the lid so that he can see the motion.

- Drop a toy in the jar and replace the lid so that it will open easily.

- Encourage him to get the toy out of the container. If he does not try to unscrew the lid, place your hand over his and open it together. *We use our hands to turn the lid. Now it's open.*

- Notice how he tries to screw the lid back on. He may just push the lid onto the container. With practice, he will be able to use his hand to successfully turn and close the lid.

- Talk about what he is doing. *You're turning the lid to close it.*

- Provide time for him to play with the containers, lids, and toys while he practices his new skill.

Let's read together!

Elephants on Board
by Suse MacDonald

Ready to move on?

Give your child several small containers with various kinds of lids. Give him small objects to put in the containers. Offer direction when needed, but let him choose how to play with the objects. Talk to him about the choices he is making. *You put the small lid on the small jar and the big lid on the big jar!*

Beginning to Share

> This one is yours, and this one is Robbie's.

> Can you give Robbie his banana?

Notice and talk about all the ways your child is beginning to share.

Your talk will give him ideas and words to use later when he begins to form friendships with other children.

Why this is important

A toddler does not know how to take turns, divide snacks, or give away toys he wants. He must learn that sharing means giving freely by choice. He may not consistently behave generously for many years, but with practice he will learn early that sharing can be a pleasant experience. Encouraging your child to share feelings and objects with you provides your child with a pattern for later sharing ideas and materials with friends.

What you do

● Model sharing by being physically near when your child plays. Offer to let him park his small car on your knee, or let him hide a block in your pocket.

● Encourage him to share his toys with you by asking questions about them and touching them. If he offers it to you, thank him and hold the toy briefly before returning it to him.

● Help him practice sharing with others by giving him two of something. Tell him one is for him and the other is for a friend or family member. *This graham cracker is yours and this one is for Daddy. Can you give it to him?*

● Make each sharing experience a positive one by focusing on the generosity he shows and describing why it was good to share. *Thank you for sharing the graham crackers with Daddy. He was hungry, too, just like you.*

Another idea

Look for opportunities to share throughout your day together. Your child can pick wildflowers for a neighbor or offer a toy to a pet.

Let's read together!

How Kind!
by Mary Murphy

Exploring Outdoors

Do those flowers smell nice?

Describe the things your child points to or picks up while you play with her outside.

This helps your child to understand the world and learn new words to use as she talks about her experiences.

Here's a yellow leaf. Do you want to hold it?

Why this is important

Playing outdoors gives your child endless ideas for play. Walking and talking with her while outdoors encourages her to explore with confidence. As you describe the things she points to or picks up, you are teaching her words she can use later to talk about her experiences. You are also helping her understand the world around her.

What you do

- Walk outside with your child and encourage her to explore and investigate. Help her feel confident by making sure she is safe while outside.

- Talk about what she sees and touches. *The grass feels cool. That's a prickly bush!*

- Look for any interesting object to share and talk about with your child. *Look at that yellow dandelion.*

- Invite her to safely touch and examine leaves, flowers, sticks, sand, or rocks. She may want you to carry a few items she collects. If she smells a flower, ask her how it smells. When in the sandbox, allow her to play freely as you sit nearby to watch.

- Describe her play using words such as *gritty, sweet, slippery, rough, smooth, scoop, dig, between your fingers,* etc.

Another idea

Add variety to her outdoor play by exploring different places. Simply crossing the street offers new opportunities for your child to explore.

Let's read together!

Pie in the Sky
by Lois Ehlert

How Does It Feel?

> *Does that sandpaper feel scratchy?*

> *You found a smooth ball in the bag!*

Invite your child to feel a few objects and then find them by touch when they are out of sight.

Your child will begin to connect the words you say with the textures he touches.

Why this is important

Your child will enjoy touching objects with different textures. When he learns the words that describe the way an object feels, he will develop a better understanding of that object. Asking him to use his sense of touch to find an object gives him practice with following directions.

What you do

- Place three or four objects of varying textures in a box. A few examples are: a cotton ball, a pinecone, a hairbrush, a ball, sandpaper, and a crayon.

- Encourage your child to open the box and feel the objects.

- Talk about each item as he explores it. *That's a cotton ball. It's very soft.* Always use the same word to describe the same texture. Use more than one object of a particular texture so that your child understands that *soft* is not the name of the object but a word to describe an object.

- Give him plenty of time to explore the objects. Then, place two of the objects in a bag so that your child can no longer see them.

- Ask him to find one of the objects by reaching in to look for it using only his fingers. He may try to use his eyes to find the object. Encourage him to try again with his hands. *Let's see if you can find it with your fingers. Find a ball that's round and smooth.*

- Repeat the game using the same objects until he can intentionally choose the one you ask for.

- Add another object to the bag. If he is having success, work up to three or four items at a time.

Another idea

Ask him to locate an object by only giving him a description of the object, not the name. *Can you find something scratchy? Can you find something hard?*

Let's read together!

Dog
by Matthew Van Fleet and Brian Stanton

Painting With Water

You made a mark with the sponge!

Encourage your child to explore what happens when he rubs a wet sponge on different surfaces.

You will be giving your child a chance to direct his own play and discover that he has the ability to change his environment.

THE
CREATIVE CURRICULUM®
LearningGames®

Why this is important

For young children, each new activity provides chances for decision making and creativity. By experimenting with water and sponges, he will begin to notice changes his actions make to the environment. Self-directed play helps your child develop confidence in his ability to make decisions. Holding the sponge and moving his hand and arm in a purposeful way to make marks are good practice for later when he will hold a pencil for writing.

What you do

- Find a place where your child can paint with water and you will not have to worry about the mess. An outside wall or sidewalk work well.

- Fill a bucket, no more than halfway, with water, and find a sponge that your child can easily hold in his hand.

- Show him how to dip the sponge into the water and squeeze before he begins painting.

- Point out the wet surface he creates. *You made a line on the wall!* Allow him to decide what to paint next.

- Notice how your child begins to control his movements in order to direct the sponge in a specific way. He may try different arm movements to create different strokes with the sponge. He might also become more interested in the sponge and practice dipping it in the bucket and squeezing out the excess water. Let him direct the activity.

Another idea

If your child needs a few suggestions of what to paint on, let him try steps, tree trunks, or rocks. In the house, the kitchen floor is a good surface. You can offer him a paintbrush with a bowl of water and let him paint a few toys and plastic dishes.

Let's read together!

Olivia
by Ian Falconer

Scribbling

You made a blue circle with your crayon.

Talk to your child about his actions, the marks he makes, and the feelings he shows as he uses a crayon.

Your child will explore the hand and finger control that will help him repeat or vary the marks he makes on the paper.

Why this is important

As your toddler experiments with making simple strokes and scribbles with crayons, he is learning to control his hand and make deliberate marks. As his ability to control the crayon grows, he is able to repeat his marks and change them. Gaining control of hand and finger motions is a necessary step in getting ready for writing. Allowing him to decide how to draw develops creativity and imagination.

What you do

- Sit with your child at a table with crayons and a large piece of paper taped to the table. Invite him to choose a crayon and begin marking the paper. Watch quietly until he finishes, then comment on his work. *You made a straight blue line!*

- Recreate a line he has drawn using your own piece of paper. *You made a red, curvy line. I think I will try to make one like you did.*

- Talk about any broad movements he makes with his arm. If he draws a spiral, point out how his arm goes around and around. Imitate his movement as you draw your own spiral.

- Notice your child making smaller, more controlled lines. *You put that line just where you wanted it.*

- Keep the sessions short, but keep drawing materials handy so that he can return to them frequently.

Ready to move on?

Point out any marks that resemble letters. *This line curves like the letter C.*

Let's read together!

Harold and the Purple Crayon
by Crockett Johnson

Trying New Motions

You're taking careful steps.

Show your child how to walk sideways, backward, or across a low bridge.

Your child's skill level and confidence will increase as he learns to control his body while moving in challenging ways.

THE
CREATIVE CURRICULUM®
LearningGames®

Why this is important

Your toddler is now able to take on several new physical skills. He will learn that he can move his body in new ways. Learning how to coordinate different motions will help him with activities such as riding a tricycle or swinging.

What you do

- Walk a few steps backward while your toddler watches you. Talk about the movement. *I'm walking backward. Would you like to hold my hand and walk backward, too?*

- Try walking sideways together, or crawling on your hands and knees.

- Make a bridge from a wide board and two bricks. Help him stand on one end, then go to the other end and encourage him to walk to you. Hold his hand if needed, and offer positive feedback when he reaches the other end. *You made it to the other side!*

Another idea

Sing songs to offer another way for your child to try new movements. *If you're happy and you know it turn around.*

Let's read together!

If You're Happy and You Know It, Clap Your Hands!
by David Carter

Matching Colors

Which sock looks the same as the one on your foot?

Can you find one like this?

Help your child match two like-colored objects in a group of three.

Hearing you say the names of colors as she selects them helps her to later identify and sort objects by color.

Why this is important

Drawing your child's attention to colors helps her learn the names of each one, match and group items of identical color, and notice the differences between colors. Your child may find it easier to understand and remember an object if she can place it in a category such as color.

What you do

● Draw your child's attention to the colors of objects as she plays with them. *Find three objects with two being the same color.* Use the words *like* and *same.*

● Show her the three objects. Choose one, show it to her, and ask her to find the other one that is the same color. *I have a yellow block. Look at the colors. Can you find one like mine?*

● Describe her choice and offer her another try if she chooses the wrong color. *That block is red. My block is yellow. Can you find another yellow block?*

● Give her time to find the matching item. If she still does not, then place your object next to the correct one. *Look at the yellow blocks. They are the same.* Stop playing if she appears frustrated.

● Move the objects on the table as you play, so that she has to look in a new spot each time. When she finds the matching object, even accidentally, offer her encouragement. *You found the yellow block just like mine!*

● Invite her to lead the game and ask you to choose a block. She may vary the game by stacking the blocks or hiding them.

Ready to move on?

Add more blocks, and more colors, to the game once your child can easily choose between two or three colors. Encourage her to group objects by color. Offer her a tray or box to help separate the objects by color.

Let's read together!

Mouse Paint
by Ellen Stoll Walsh

Using Tools

You're using the spoon to help you reach the block!

Encourage your child to use an object as a tool to get an item that is out of reach.

Your child will practice using tools to solve problems.

THE CREATIVE CURRICULUM®
LearningGames®

Why this is important

When you encourage your child to use objects to reach things, she learns that tools can help her complete tasks she could not otherwise do. When she uses a wooden spoon to move a block closer to her, she learns that an object such as a spoon can be used in more than one way. This understanding helps her think of new ways to solve problems.

What you do

- Look for opportunities to offer your child a tool to use to get something that is out of reach. For example, when her ball rolls under a chair and out of her reach, use the opportunity to offer her a tool that can help her get the ball. Give her a ruler to reach with. Be sure to supervise her exploration and give her some help if needed.

- Place a few blocks out of her reach on a table. Place a long wooden spoon on the table and wait to see if she will use the spoon as a tool. Help her by asking, *Can you use the spoon to reach the blocks?*

- Show your child other tools to use such as a low, sturdy stool to help her reach high places. When using the stool, make sure you have removed dangerous items to another room or a very high shelf. **A stool should be used only if you are able to watch and help as your child uses it.**

- Step back and let her discover new uses for household objects. She may surprise you with her ideas!

Another idea

Encourage your child to help with household chores so she can see how you use tools around the house. Offer her a wagon to use to collect her toys at clean-up time.

Let's read together!

Tools
by Ann Morris

See, Show, Say

Show me a purple lunchbox.

As you read with your child, invite her to look at, point to, and talk about what she sees on the page.

Reading interactively helps your child stay interested in a book and learn.

Why this is important

Young children who pay close attention to and talk about books are more engaged in learning. Engaging your child in the story helps increase her vocabulary and comprehension, which are important early literacy skills.

What you do

- Sit comfortably with your child to establish a loving reading routine. Pay attention to her eyes as you read a familiar book. If she looks at something on the page when you read about it, pause and describe it. *You see that big, red truck.*

- Continue to read her favorite books to her. As long as she is actively looking and listening she will be learning from the experience.

- Invite her to participate during reading. *There is a bicycle. Can you put your finger on the bicycle?* Or, *Which coat is blue? Can you find the blue coat?* Encourage her to repeat a few words such as *blue* or *coat.*

- Ask questions when she feels comfortable with the book. *What is the little boy holding? Where do you think they are going?* Give your child time to talk about the picture before moving on.

- Think of seeing, showing, and saying as three levels of response to a story, each one more challenging than the last. Start a new book with simply asking your child to notice the pictures. On pages where she cannot name objects, invite her to point. If she can say the names of the objects, ask questions so she will answer with words and not actions.

Another idea

Give your child time to ask questions about the book. Answer her questions in ways that extend her involvement with the book. *The fire truck is going to put out the fire. Let's make the sound of the siren together. Rrrr.*

Let's read together!

Find the Puppy
by Phil Roxbee Cox